LEADERSHIP AND INNOVATION

FOSTERING A CULTURE OF CREATIVITY

DANIEL NJUGUNA

DEDICATION

This book is devoted to everyone who has the guts to drive innovation, foster a culture of ideas, and lead with creativity. This work is an homage to your dedication to excellence, to the visionary leaders who are boldly and resiliently defining the future, and to the teams whose collaborative spirit powers the engine of growth.

May the information in these pages open your eyes, stimulate your creative thinking, and enable leaders and innovators to pave the route for success in the ever-changing field of creativity.

With appreciation and thanks,

[Daniel W. Njuguna]

CONTENTS

ACKNOWLEDGMENTS

Upon the completion of "Leadership and Innovation: Fostering a Culture of Creativity," I am incredibly appreciative of all the people who have made this project possible.

Sincere gratitude is owed to the editorial and publishing teams, which include the editors, proofreaders, and designers. Their knowledge and commitment have turned the manuscript into a polished and eye-catching finished work.

I appreciate all the friends, coworkers, and mentors who have supported and encouraged me along the way. Your insight, support, and readiness to conduct thought-provoking conversations have had a lasting impression on this work.

I want to express my gratitude to my family and friends for their constant support and patience over the long hours I spent researching and writing. I sincerely appreciate your love and inspiration, and your patience and support have been my pillars.

Lastly, I want to thank the readers of "Leadership and Innovation." Your interest in and participation in the concepts discussed in these pages is the last confirmation of our collective efforts.

This book is the outcome of a team effort, and I am grateful for the help and input from all the people listed above. I hope the concepts discussed in these pages stimulate and add to the current conversation on innovation and leadership.

With sincere gratitude,

[Daniel W. Njuguna]

[Author]

1 INTRODUCTION

1.1 Leadership in the Twenty-First Century

In this pivotal section, the exploration of leadership transcends conventional boundaries, encompassing the following key elements:

• **Adaptability:** Leadership in the twenty-first century necessitates a shift away from rigid, top-down institutions. Instead, leaders must embrace adaptation as they navigate the intricacies of a rapidly changing global landscape.

• **Emotional Intelligence:** In addition to technical capabilities, influential leaders have vital emotional intelligence, understanding and controlling their own emotions and the feelings of their team members. This improves communication, collaboration, and team relations.

• **Global Awareness:** Leaders in the current era must be acutely aware of the world's interdependence. A global perspective is critical for navigating varied cultural landscapes, fostering inclusivity, and making informed decisions in a quickly changing global context.

• **Technical Fluency:** Today's leadership requires a certain amount of technical fluency. Leaders must be able to navigate and leverage technology to generate innovation, efficiency, and organizational success.

• **Strategic Vision:** Leaders must see beyond day-to-day operations in the twenty-first century. They are strategic vision architects capable of steering their organizations toward long-term goals while adjusting to changing circumstances.

• **Inclusive Leadership:** Effective leadership requires the recognition and celebration of diversity. Inclusive leaders foster cultures where people from all walks of life feel respected, contributing to a rich tapestry of opinions and ideas.

This part is a basic inquiry, establishing the foundations for understanding the multidimensional character of modern leadership. It establishes the tone for the next chapters, in which these distinguishing features are further dissected and applied in the context of encouraging innovation and creativity.

1.2 The Critical Relationship Between Leadership and Innovation

This section delves deeper into the relationship between successful leadership and the fostering of innovation. It entails the following:

• **Visionary Leadership:** Leaders are critical to delivering a clear vision that corresponds with company goals. This vision serves as a beacon, inspiring individuals and teams to think beyond the status quo and seek innovative solutions.

• **Cultural Catalysts:** Leaders serve as catalysts in the development of a corporate culture that promotes creativity and innovation. They set the tone by encouraging risk-taking, viewing failure as a learning opportunity, and developing an openness to new ideas.

• **Empowerment:** Skilled leaders enable their groups to express their creative ideas with confidence by giving them freedom and fostering an atmosphere of support. Empowerment like this fosters a dedication to creative projects and a sense of ownership.

• **Resource Allocation:** In order to foster creative endeavors, leaders must strategically allocate resources, including people, money, and time. They give projects that support the organization's long-term innovation goals top priority and invest in them.

• **Open Communication:** Open communication is essential to the growth of an innovative culture. To dismantle organizational silos and promote cross-functional innovation, leaders create a collaborative atmosphere where ideas are freely shared and constructive criticism is welcomed.

• **Adaptation to Change:** Being a leader means guiding the group through transition. In order to navigate the organization through the uncertainties brought on by innovation, technological advancements, and changes in the business landscape, leaders need to be flexible and agile.

This exploration highlights how important leadership is in fostering an environment where creativity thrives. These ideas will be further explained in the upcoming chapters.

1.3 Putting Things in Perspective: The State of Creativity in Organizations Today

This section examines the current state of creativity in organizational contexts to set the stage for our exploration. This is detailed as follows:

• **Obstacles to Creativity:** Bureaucratic roadblocks, opposition to change, and a fear of failing are just a few of the difficulties organizations face when trying to promote creativity. Establishing an atmosphere that supports innovation requires recognizing and addressing these issues.

• **Innovation Opportunities:** In the face of difficulties, businesses can seize the chance to unleash latent creative potential. Innovative thinking can be stimulated by embracing diversity, promoting interdisciplinary collaboration, and utilizing technology advancements.

• **Technological Influence:** Technology has a big say in how the creative environment is shaped. Companies need to use tools and platforms to boost their creative processes and maintain their competitiveness as they adjust to the quick speed at which technology is developing.

• **Cultural Aspects:** The culture of an organization is crucial in fostering creativity. A vibrant creative environment is facilitated by a culture that values experimentation, promotes diversity of thought, and honors and rewards creative work.

• **Global Dynamics:** Understanding the global dynamics of creativity is crucial in a world of interconnected economies. Organizations must understand international collaborations, cultural quirks, and trends as they may affect their creative endeavors.

• **Strategic Importance:** Promoting a creative culture is not only a desirable but also a necessary strategic move. Organizations that prioritize and invest in creativity are better positioned for long-term success, as creativity is increasingly acknowledged as a driver of competitive advantage.

This section functions as a diagnostic analysis, pinpointing the major factors influencing the state of creativity in organizations today. In order to prepare for the upcoming chapters, which will examine strategies for overcoming obstacles and seizing opportunities, it invites reflection on the opportunities and challenges that organizations face as they set out to cultivate a culture of creativity.

2 THE DEVELOPMENT OF LEADERSHIP STYLES

2.1 Traditional Leadership Models: Advantages and Drawbacks

This section explores the fundamental elements of conventional leadership models, recognizing their advantages as well as disadvantages. This is explained below:

Advantages:

• **Clear Hierarchy:** Roles and responsibilities are clearly defined in a hierarchical structure provided by traditional models. An environment at work that is stable and well-organized may benefit from this clarity.

• **Command and Control:** In some circumstances, a command-and-control strategy may work well, especially in sectors where accuracy, productivity, and consistency are critical.

• **Predictability:** Routine and predictability are frequently emphasized in traditional models, which can be helpful in stable environments where deviating from set procedures can result in inefficiencies.

• **Established Processes:** Conventional leadership models are frequently linked to precise protocols and guidelines that offer consistency and organization.

Drawbacks:

• **Resistance to Change:** When faced with Change, traditional models' rigidity can cause resistance. Being unable to adapt can make it more difficult to be innovative and responsive in quickly changing environments.

• **Limited Employee Engagement:** Employee empowerment and engagement may be restricted as a result of strict hierarchies. This lack of participation can inhibit innovation and reduce team members' sense of ownership.

• **Slow Decision-Making:** Time-consuming hierarchical decision-making procedures is a major challenge. In circumstances where promptness and flexibility are essential, the bureaucratic structure of conventional models may pose an obstacle.

• **Top-Down Communication:** Most communication occurs at the top level, which can impede open communication and prevent team members from freely exchanging ideas.

This analysis lays the groundwork for a nuanced understanding of traditional leadership models, appreciating their benefits while also acknowledging the limitations they might have in the modern world, which calls for creativity and adaptability. As we go, we'll look at different leadership philosophies that tackle the drawbacks of conventional models and take into account the changing demands of 21st-century businesses.

2.2 Adaptive Leadership: Navigating Change in a Dynamic Environment

This section focuses on adaptive leadership, a flexible strategy that can be used to manage the challenges of a world that is changing quickly. It involves various features:

Principal Features:
• **Flexibility**: Adaptive leadership places a strong emphasis on

adapting to change. In response to changing conditions, leaders need to be flexible enough to change course, adopt new tactics, and accept new ideas.

• **Learning Orientation**: An adaptable leader cultivates a mindset of constant learning for both themselves and their groups. This calls for a readiness to try new things, learn from mistakes, and modify plans in response to criticism.

• **Collaborative Problem-Solving:** Adaptive leaders promote inclusivity and teamwork when solving problems. They understand that different viewpoints foster creative thinking, particularly when faced with uncertainty.

• **Resilience**: It takes resilience to navigate Change. Adaptive leaders foster resilience within their teams by offering assistance, admitting difficulties, and keeping a positive attitude despite difficult circumstances.

Navigating Change:

• **Anticipating Change**: Proactively preparing their teams for future developments, adaptable leaders anticipate shifts in the external environment.

• **Quickness in Making Decisions**: Agile decision-making in adaptive leadership enables prompt reactions to new opportunities or dangers. This is in contrast to traditional models' frequently sluggish decision-making processes.

• **Empowering Teams**: Adaptive leaders cultivate an environment of accountability and autonomy in order to empower their teams. The empowerment of the team improves its capacity to adapt efficiently to changing circumstances.

• **Embracing Uncertainty**: Adaptable Leaders recognize and welcome uncertainty. They give their teams a sense of confidence and purpose by seeing Change as an opportunity for growth rather than a threat.

This examination of adaptive leadership lays the groundwork for comprehending leadership philosophies that are more in line with the needs of a constantly evolving and dynamic world. We'll explore how adaptive leadership concepts can be used to encourage creativity and innovation in businesses in the following sections.

2.3 Transformational Leadership: Encouraging Creativity on All Fronts

The emphasis in this section is on transformational leadership, a management approach that goes beyond traditional methods to stimulate significant Change and innovation. This is detailed below:

Crucial Features:

• **Visionary Leadership**: Leaders who are transformational offer an inspiring vision that extends beyond daily tasks. This vision is a potent source of inspiration, encouraging people to pursue greatness and welcome innovation.

• **Charismatic Influence**: Teams are captivated and motivated by the charismatic influence of transformational leaders. Their contagious enthusiasm and passion inspire a sense of purpose and dedication in others.

• **Individualized Consideration**: Transformational leaders consider each team member based on their strengths and needs. This kind of approach fosters growth on both a personal and professional level and establishes trust.

• **Intellectual Stimulation**: By promoting creativity and critical thinking, these leaders help to stimulate the mind. They oppose the status quo and foster an atmosphere that values fresh perspectives and fosters curiosity.

Promoting Innovation:

• **Encouraging Creativity**: Transformational leaders encourage their groups to take chances and think creatively. They foster an environment where people are encouraged to try out new ideas and where failure is viewed as a teaching opportunity.

• **Fostering an Innovative Culture**: Transformational leaders help to create an environment where innovation is not only welcomed but actively encouraged by highlighting an innovative vision. This Change in culture affects the organization at all levels.

• **Promoting Collaboration**: Transformational leaders encourage cooperation by dismantling organizational silos and creating a setting where various viewpoints come together to produce creative solutions.

• **Continuous Improvement**: Transformational leadership is inherently devoted to constant improvement. Leaders inspire their teams to continuously evaluate themselves and look for better ways to accomplish tasks.

This examination of transformational leadership sheds light on how it can stimulate innovation by promoting a culture that values innovation, teamwork, and constant improvement. As we go along, we'll explore real-world applications and doable tactics for incorporating the ideas of transformational leadership into organizational structures.

3 UNLOCKING THE POTENTIAL FOR CREATIVITY

3.1 Fostering an Inventive Mentality

This section turns to the most important component of helping people and teams develop a creative mindset. This can be achieved through the following ways:

Embracing Curiosity: Developing curiosity is the first step towards developing a creative mindset. People who have a creative mindset, are inherently curious, and want to learn about and comprehend the world they live in. In order to develop and encourage this curiosity among their teams, leaders are essential.

Promoting Divergent Thinking: Divergent thinking is the capacity to examine various viewpoints and solutions in order to develop a creative mindset. Leaders cultivate a culture that recognizes the richness of differing points of View by establishing an atmosphere in which different ideas are not only accepted but actively sought after.

Taking Risks and Accepting Failure: An environment that promotes taking risks and views Failure as a necessary step toward success is conducive to creativity. By encouraging a culture where measured risks are welcomed and failure lessons are celebrated, leaders can help people overcome their fear of failing.

Creating Autonomy: People who feel like they have some control over their lives tend to think more creatively. By giving their team members the latitude to try new things, explore, and take responsibility for their work, leaders enable their followers. This autonomy encourages accountability and responsibility, two qualities that are essential to fostering creativity.

Cross-disciplinary Collaboration: The nexus of various disciplines is where creativity arises. Cross-disciplinary collaboration is facilitated by leaders who provide chances for people with different backgrounds and skill sets to interact, exchange ideas, and jointly develop creative solutions.

Time and Space for Reflection: Making time and space for reflection is essential to fostering a creative mindset. Leaders understand that giving people the space to take a step back, consider their work, and make connections between seemingly unrelated ideas is essential for coming up with fresh and creative ideas.

Ongoing Education and Skill Development: By encouraging a culture of ongoing education, leaders cultivate a creative mindset. A dynamic and forward-thinking workplace is created by supporting team members' professional development, skill acquisition, and exploration of new trends. This examination of developing a creative mindset highlights how important leadership is in influencing the attitudes and actions that promote creativity.

We'll look at doable approaches to incorporating these ideas into organizational procedures as we go.

3.2 Fostering an Inclusive and Diverse Culture

This section's emphasis switches to how crucial it is to create a diverse and welcoming culture in order to encourage innovation and creativity. This can be attained through the following ways:

Recognizing Diversity: Developing an inclusive and varied culture begins with having a solid understanding of diversity. Leaders understand that diversity includes differences in viewpoints, experiences, and ways of thinking, in addition to demographic differences.

Appreciating Inclusivity: Inclusivity is more than just having a diverse workforce; it's about fostering an atmosphere in which each person is treated with respect and feels important. Leaders promote inclusivity as a core value of the company's culture.

Breaking Down Bias: Identifying and eradicating biases within the organization is an active task for leaders. Biases in the hiring, promotion, and Decision-making processes fall into this category. A more equal workplace is facilitated by raising awareness of unconscious biases and offering training on them.

Encouraging Equal Opportunities: Encouraging an inclusive culture in an organization means giving equal opportunities to everyone. Leaders make sure that everyone has equal access to resources, Mentorship and career advancement opportunities, regardless of identity or background.

Promoting a Culture of Belonging: An inclusive and diverse culture is one in which each person has a sense of community. By fostering forums for candid discussion, recognizing the value of different viewpoints, and taking proactive measures to address any instances of exclusion or discrimination, leaders foster a sense of belonging.

Promoting Diversity of Thought: Leaders understand that a diverse range of Perspectives can spur creativity. Leaders can access a multitude of perspectives that stimulate innovative problem-solving by creating an atmosphere where people feel free to voice their distinct opinions.

Enacting Inclusive Policies: Leaders advocate for the creation and execution of laws that actively advance inclusivity. This includes programs that cater to the unique needs of various employee groups, training on diversity and inclusion, and flexible work schedules.

Measuring and Monitoring Inclusion: Leaders are aware that management follows
measurement. They create metrics to gauge inclusivity, evaluate

diversity and inclusion programs on a regular basis, and use the information to guide decision-making for ongoing development. This examination of creating an inclusive and diverse culture highlights critical role that leadership plays in creating a setting where people feel empowered to share their viewpoints and, eventually, develop an atmosphere that encourages creativity and innovation. As we continue, we will explore tactics for putting diversity and inclusion initiatives into practice and keeping them going within organizations.

3.3 Overcoming Mental Blocks: Overcoming Opposition to Change

This section focuses on comprehending and overcoming the psychological obstacles that frequently go along with resistance to change inside an organization. Its success factors comprise the following:

Identifying Cognitive Biases: Leaders are aware of the cognitive biases that influence resistance. Common biases like status quo bias and loss aversion can produce mental obstacles. Leaders are better equipped to deal with these biases when they are aware of them.

Openness and Communication: Having effective Communication is essential to overcoming mental obstacles. Transparent leaders address concerns and highlight the advantages of change while outlining the reasons for it. The open exchange of ideas reduces anxiety about the unknown and promotes trust.

Creating a Sense of Urgency: By outlining the necessity of change, leaders foster a sense of urgency. Leaders inspire people to embrace change and get out of their comfort zones by highlighting how important it is to adjust to changing circumstances or take advantage of new opportunities.

Promoting a Growth Mindset: A growth mindset—the belief that knowledge and abilities may be acquired via challenges—is necessary to overcome resistance. Leaders foster an environment that values growth and learning in order to support this way of thinking. Identifying and empowering change champions within the organization is the responsibility of leaders. These people, who are enthusiastic about the suggested modifications, can positively influence their peers and act as role models for accepting novel approaches to thinking and doing.

Handling the Fear of the Unknown: This mental obstacle is frequently caused by a fear of the unknown. By giving as much information as they can about the upcoming changes, providing support and training, and highlighting the possible benefits, leaders can help to reduce this anxiety.

Inclusive Decision-Making: Including staff members in the process of making decisions lessens opposition. By soliciting feedback, paying attention to issues, and taking into account different viewpoints, leaders encourage a sense of responsibility and engagement among their staff.

Rewarding Little Victories: Progress is reinforced when small victories are recognized and celebrated during the transformation process. Leaders foster a positive momentum that promotes continued adaptation by acknowledging and appreciating the contributions of both individuals and teams.

This examination of breaking through mental obstacles emphasizes how important leadership is in helping people go through the process of change. Leaders can establish a more flexible and creative organizational culture by comprehending and addressing the psychological components of resistance. We will go into more detail as we go along about how to manage change in organizations practically.

4 CREATING A VISIONARY ORGANIZATION

4.1 The Function of Vision in Advancing Innovation

In this section, we explore the importance of compelling vision and the role of visionary leadership in promoting innovation. It is crucial in the following ways:

A guiding light for innovation: Innovation is guided by a distinct and motivating vision. It gives people a sense of direction, bringing teams and individuals together around a single objective. An organization's mission is encapsulated in a vision that leaders articulate, and they also ignite creativity and a shared commitment to innovative endeavors.

Inspiration for Creativity: By presenting a clear picture of the future, visionary leaders stimulate creativity. The vision acts as a source of motivation, inspiring people to look beyond the current problems and imagine creative solutions that advance the achievement of the larger objectives.

Alignment with Organizational Values: An organization's core values should be reflected in the vision statement, as this will create a culture in which innovation is not just a strategic initiative but a fundamental part of the organization's identity. It brings the organization's values, mission, and pursuit of innovative solutions into harmony.

Risk-Taking Motivation: Innovation frequently necessitates taking measured risks. A compelling vision inspires people to embrace risk-taking and leave their comfort zones in order to realize the goals of the vision. Leaders convey that the organization's overarching vision is in line with the pursuit of innovation.

Promoting a long-term outlook: Leadership with vision cultivates a long-term outlook on innovation. While short-term objectives are crucial, leaders and teams are inspired to approach innovation strategically by a compelling vision that takes the organization's sustainability and future success into account.

Creating a Shared Vision: Skilled leaders make sure that the vision is a shared aspiration rather than a top-down directive. They instill a sense of ownership by involving teams in the conception and development of the vision. This common vision catalyzes the bringing of disparate viewpoints together in pursuit of creative goals.

Adaptability in the Vision: A vision that can change course in response to evolving conditions is necessary in a creative and dynamic environment. Recognizing the importance of adaptability, visionary leaders periodically review and enhance the vision to guarantee its pertinence and congruence with new prospects and obstacles.

Communication of Purpose: Putting the vision into actionable steps requires effective communication. Effective leaders make the vision tangible and relevant to people at all organizational levels by effectively communicating its purpose. This transparency gives rise to a purposeful mindset that stimulates creativity.

This investigation highlights the critical role that visionary leadership plays in cultivating an innovative culture. As we progress, we'll go deeper into the ways that leaders can effectively convey their vision and carry it out in order to foster and maintain innovative practices inside their companies.

4.2 Presenting an Enthralling Vision: Motivating Groups to Think Outside the Box

This section centers on the skill and significance of skillfully conveying an inspiring vision to motivate teams to push beyond traditional boundaries. The following ways can be applied:

Simplicity and Clarity: Simplicity and clarity are the foundations of an effective vision communication strategy. To ensure that every member of the team understands the overall aim and its relevance, leaders condense the substance of the vision into language that is easily understood.

Using stories as a tool: Storytelling develops into an effective communication technique. Leaders craft stories that put the vision in perspective and amplify its emotional resonance. Narratives captivate the imagination, establishing a bond that surpasses conventional tactical goals.

Graphical Illustration: Making use of visual components improves the conveying of an engaging vision. Visual aids like infographics and charts make difficult concepts easier to understand and retain, which increases the impact and memory of the vision.

Involvement and Conversation: Leaders and their teams actively participate in dialogue, promoting inquiries, debates, and criticism. Team members have a sense of inclusion and value in their ideas as they work toward the vision, thanks to this interactive method.

Pertinence to Specific Roles: Team members need to know how their individual duties and functions fit into the larger picture. To create a feeling of purpose and involvement, leaders customize their communication to show how the team's everyday duties relate to the vision.

Consistent reinforcement: A compelling vision is a narrative that changes and adapts rather than a one-time declaration. The vision is constantly reaffirmed by leaders, who include it in team meetings, project updates, and other forms of communication. Repetition improves comprehension and dedication.

Alignment with values: Leaders highlight the alignment between the organization's basic values and the vision. The conviction that pursuing the vision is more than just a calculated action and instead an expression of the organization's values is strengthened by this alignment, which fosters a sense of authenticity and integrity.

Acknowledging Milestones: Highlighting the vision's accomplishments and benchmarks helps keep it moving forward. By praising team members' contributions, leaders establish a positive feedback loop that encourages sustained dedication to the main goal.

This investigation highlights the fact that communication is a dynamic, continuous process that converts an inspiring vision into useful inspiration. In the future, we'll go into more detail on how leaders may create an environment that encourages individuals to think outside the box and take the initiative to realize the common goal.

4.3 Matching Creative Objectives with Organizational Goals

This section centers on the strategic alignment of creative objectives and organizational goals, fostering a mutually beneficial link between innovation and the larger mission. This is done through the following ways:

Integration of strategy: Strategic integration of innovation into the overarching mission is necessary to align corporate goals with creative objectives. Effective leaders make sure that innovation is a core component of the organization's strategic plan, not just a side project.

Outlining Specific Creative Goals: Leaders articulate creative goals that are in line with the organization's objectives in a clear and precise manner. These goals function as concrete benchmarks that facilitate the accomplishment of more expansive strategic plans.

Incorporating Originality into Goal-Setting: Leaders

intentionally include creativity as a crucial element when defining organizational goals. This integration makes sure that innovation is viewed as a vital component of company success rather than as a stand-alone entity.

Balancing Short-Term and Long-Term Goals: Leaders that are effective balance immediate and long-term goals. They take into account how creative initiatives contribute to the organization's long-term sustainability and growth, in addition to meeting urgent demands.

Collaboration Across Functions: Cross-functional cooperation is necessary to achieve organizational goals that prioritize creativity. In order to achieve innovative goals, leaders cultivate a collaborative culture that dismantles departmental silos and maximizes synergies.

Allocating Resources to Foster Creativity: Leaders do strategic resource allocation to assist innovative projects. This includes monetary outlays, committed staff members, and technological infrastructure. The organization's dedication to promoting an innovative culture is reflected in the distribution of resources.

Measuring and Evaluating Creative Impact: Setting up measures to gauge the effectiveness of creative goals is essential. In order to provide data-driven insights for plans, leaders put assessment processes in place to evaluate how creative endeavors contribute to the accomplishment of company goals.

Ongoing Adaptation: A dedication to ongoing adaptation is necessary for the alignment of creative aspirations with corporate goals. Leaders continue to be adaptable, changing tactics in response to changes in the organization's and the industry's overall environment.

This exploration highlights how there is a real and strategic integration—rather than just an aspirational one—between creative ambitions and corporate goals. As we go along, we'll look more closely at how executives might successfully negotiate the complexities of coordinating creativity with broad organizational plans.

5 MANAGING EFFECTIVE INNOVATION TEAMS

5.1 Establishing and Maintaining Multidisciplinary Teams

The creation and upkeep of cross-functional teams are the key topics of this section, with an emphasis on cooperation and synergy across a range of skill sets. This is detailed below:

Varying Skill Sets: Cross-functional teams unite people with different backgrounds, specialties, and skill sets. This diversity enhances the team's combined knowledge and skills, which is a vital strength.

Dismantling Silos: The creation of cross-functional teams breaks down conventional organizational silos. These teams break down boundaries that frequently impede innovation by bringing together personnel from various departments or specialties to promote open communication and collaboration.

Shared Objective: A cross-functional team works toward a common purpose that complements the objectives of the company. This shared goal unites the team and directs its efforts toward a particular result that advances the mission as a whole.

Skillful Communication: Within cross-functional teams, effective communication is essential. Leaders make sure that team members are able to exchange information easily, fostering an atmosphere where ideas are freely exchanged and criticism is actively welcomed.

Accountability and Ownership of the Project: Members of cross-functional teams assume responsibility for particular project components. People are motivated to put forth their best efforts because they feel accountable for their actions and how they directly affect the performance of the team.

Leadership Support: An essential component of helping cross-functional teams is leadership. In order to guarantee the success of the team, leaders supply the required tools, eliminate roadblocks, and provide direction. This kind of assistance fosters an atmosphere that is favorable to innovation.

Adaptability and Flexibility: Cross-functional teams work in dynamic settings that could call for regular modifications. Team members need to be flexible, and leaders should cultivate an environment that welcomes change and pushes the group to make adjustments as needed.

Ongoing Education: Working across functional boundaries naturally involves learning. Colleagues acquire knowledge from one another's experience, expanding their perspectives outside their specialized fields. The culture of constant learning raises the collective intellect of the team.

Acknowledgment and Festivity: Leaders acknowledge and applaud the accomplishments of cross-functional groups. A healthy team culture is promoted, and the value of collaboration is reinforced by acknowledging accomplishments and milestones.

This investigation highlights the fact that creating and maintaining cross-functional teams involves more than just putting together a varied group of individuals; it also entails creating an atmosphere that promotes cooperation, clear communication, and a common dedication to accomplishing creative objectives. We will explore tactics for maximizing cross-functional teams' capacity to stimulate organizational innovation and creativity as we move forward.

5.2 Nurturing a Collaborative Environment

In this section, the focus is on creating and fostering a collaborative environment within the organization, cultivating a culture where teamwork and shared creativity thrive. This is explained below:

Open communication channels: A collaborative environment is built on open communication. Leaders establish channels that facilitate transparent and constructive communication, ensuring that ideas, feedback, and information flow freely across all levels of the organization.

Accessible Platforms for Idea Sharing: Leaders provide accessible platforms for idea sharing. Whether through digital collaboration tools or physical spaces designed for brainstorming, the organization encourages individuals to contribute their ideas and perspectives.

Cultivating a Culture of Listening: Listening is a fundamental aspect of collaboration. Leaders cultivate a culture where active listening is valued and diverse viewpoints are respected. This inclusive approach fosters an environment where every team member feels heard and acknowledged.

Encouraging Cross-Functional Interactions: Collaboration thrives when individuals from different departments and disciplines interact regularly. Leaders encourage cross-functional interactions, creating opportunities for spontaneous idea exchanges and the emergence of innovative solutions.

Team-building Activities: Engaging in team-building exercises is essential for promoting cooperation. Leaders organize activities that promote team cohesion, trust, and understanding. These activities contribute to a positive and supportive team culture.

Celebrating Team Success: Recognition is a powerful motivator for collaboration. Leaders celebrate the successes of collaborative efforts, whether big or small, reinforcing the value of teamwork and the impact it has on achieving organizational goals.

Promoting a growth mindset: A growth mindset, where challenges are viewed as opportunities for learning and improvement, is integral to a collaborative environment. Leaders encourage a mindset that embraces change, values experimentation, and sees setbacks as stepping stones to success.

Establishing clear goals and roles: Collaboration is most effective when team members have a clear understanding of their roles and the goals they collectively aim to achieve. Leaders provide clarity on expectations, ensuring that each team member understands their contribution to the collaborative process.

Diversity and Inclusion: A collaborative environment embraces diversity and inclusion. Leaders ensure that the collaborative space is inclusive of individuals from various backgrounds, fostering a rich tapestry of perspectives and ideas.

This exploration underscores that a collaborative environment is not solely about physical proximity but, more importantly, about cultivating a mindset and culture that values teamwork, open communication, and shared goals. As we proceed, we will delve into strategies for leaders to nurture and sustain this collaborative ethos within their organizations.

5.3 Developing Team Members: Finding a Balance Between Accountability and Autonomy

This section focuses on creating a culture that promotes ownership and responsibility while empowering team members by finding a balance between autonomy and accountability. Some of the ways to achieve this include the following:

Encouraging Autonomy: Giving team members some autonomy is the first step toward their empowerment. Leaders have faith in people to take initiative, solve issues, and make decisions, as well as contribute to projects. This independence encourages creativity and a sense of ownership.

Making Expectations Clear: While granting autonomy, leaders also need to establish clear guidelines. Team members must have a clear grasp of the objectives, deadlines, and standards of quality. Well-defined expectations offer a structure that facilitates the exercise of autonomy.

Promoting taking chances: Encouraging team members to take reasonable risks is a key component of empowerment. Leaders foster an environment where people feel comfortable trying new things without worrying about unwarranted consequences, where failures are viewed as learning opportunities, and where experimentation is appreciated.

Offering assistance and resources: Empowerment involves more than just autonomy; it also calls for the provision of the required tools and assistance. Leaders make certain that their team members have the resources—tools, knowledge, and guidance—necessary to thrive in their independent pursuits.

Promoting a Culture of Learning: A culture of learning fosters the growth of empowered teams. By offering chances for knowledge exchange, skill development, and training, leaders encourage lifelong learning. Team members' capacities are improved by this learning culture, making it possible for them to overcome obstacles more skillfully.

Celebrating Success: A key component of empowerment is acknowledgment. Recognizing the accomplishments and contributions of empowered teams, leaders celebrate their victories. This positive reinforcement serves to reaffirm the importance of accountability and autonomy.

Feedback and Reflection: A feedback loop is involved in empowerment. By giving team members constructive criticism, leaders promote a culture of ongoing development. Thinking back on achievements as well as failures promotes personal and societal development.

Balancing Independence and Cooperation: Although independence is valued, cooperation is still essential. In order to ensure that team members can contribute individually and collaborate effectively toward common goals, leaders must find a balance between individual autonomy and collaborative efforts.

Consistency with organizational principles: Empowerment is consistent with the ideals of the company. By ensuring that team members' autonomy aligns with the organization's guiding principles and objectives, leaders foster a cohesive and purpose-driven work environment.

This investigation highlights the careful balancing act that leaders need to take between encouraging accountability and granting autonomy. As we move further, we will explore useful tactics that leaders may use to successfully empower their teams and foster a culture where accountability and autonomy coexist together.

6 ADAPTING TO THE DISRUPTION OF TECHNOLOGY

6.1 Adopting Digital Transformation: A Crucial Leadership Role

This section focuses on how important it is for leaders to accept digital transformation and see it as a necessary component of contemporary leadership. This is explained below:

Gaining insight into digital transformation: The act of incorporating digital technologies into every aspect of an organization and drastically changing how it operates and adds value is known as digital transformation. Executives need to be well-versed with the digital environment and how it affects their sector.

Aligning Strategically: In order to fully embrace digital transformation, technological activities must be in line with strategic goals. In order to ensure long-term success, leaders must make sure that digital plans are smoothly incorporated into the broader organizational roadmap.

Cultural Transition: The adoption of digital transformation demands a change in culture. Leaders foster a culture that values adaptability, ongoing learning, and change. Organizations must undergo this cultural shift in order to keep up with the rapid speed at which technology is developing.

Innovation centered on the customer: Leaders encourage customer-centric innovation by utilizing digital tools. Organizations may better understand customer demands, personalize experiences, and provide goods and services that live up to changing expectations thanks to digital transformation.

Making Decisions Based on Data: Leaders are empowered by massive amounts of data thanks to digital transformation. Leaders must foster a culture of data-driven decision-making, wherein strategic decisions are informed by analytics and operational efficiency is enhanced.

Integration of Technology: Seamless technological integration is necessary for a successful digital transition. Leaders supervise the application of technologies like automation, cloud computing, and artificial intelligence, making sure they complement company objectives and improve productivity.

Agile Leadership: Agile leadership is necessary for digital transformation. Leaders must be flexible, willing to try new things, and sensitive to shifting market dynamics. Agile leadership guarantees that companies can quickly adapt to changing technological environments.

Development of talent: Developing a workforce with the necessary digital skills is a prerequisite for embracing digital transformation. By funding talent development initiatives, leaders make sure that staff members get the know-how needed to navigate and utilize developing technology effectively.

Cybersecurity Considerations: As we depend more on digital technologies, cybersecurity is becoming more and more important. In an increasingly digital world, leaders give cybersecurity measures priority and put strong policies in place to safeguard organizational assets and data.

Measuring digital ROI: To calculate the return on investment (ROI) of digital efforts, leaders set up measures. This entails monitoring key performance indicators (KPIs) in order to evaluate how the digital transformation affects overall success, innovation, and organizational efficiency.

This investigation emphasizes that digital transformation necessitates visionary leadership because it is a comprehensive organizational shift rather than just a technology improvement. We will explore particular tactics and considerations as we move forward to help leaders through the challenging terrain of digital transformation.

6.2 Using New Technologies to Gain a Competitive Edge

This section centers on the strategic utilization of emerging technology by leaders to attain a competitive edge in the ever-changing corporate landscape. This can be attained through:

Assessment of the Technology Landscape: Leaders stay up-to-date on developing technologies that are pertinent to their industry and perform a thorough review of the technology landscape. Their comprehension empowers them to make knowledgeable choices regarding the integration of technology.

Adoption of Strategic Technology: Leaders strategically integrate cutting-edge technologies in line with company objectives. Adoption of technology, be it AI, blockchain, IoT, or others, is motivated by the possibility of improving productivity, creativity, and overall competitiveness.

Innovation as a Foundational Strategy: Leaders view innovation as a fundamental strategic pillar. Organizations can set themselves apart in the market by utilizing technology to create creative goods, services, or procedures that give them a competitive advantage.

Implementing Agilely: It is imperative that developing technology be implemented quickly. Leaders create agile cultures to help companies experiment with new ideas, scale successful projects effectively, and quickly adopt new technologies.

Collaboration Across Functions: Often, utilizing developing technology calls for cross-functional cooperation. To make sure that technology projects are in line with larger organizational goals, leaders foster collaboration between technology specialists, business units, and other pertinent stakeholders.

Leveraging Data to Gain Strategic Understanding: Leaders place a strong emphasis on using data strategically. Leaders make sure that the massive volumes of data generated by emerging technologies are used to obtain insights that can be put into practice. Making decisions based on data becomes essential to maintaining a competitive edge.

Technology-Based Customer-Centric Solutions: Technology is used with the needs of the customer in mind. Leaders use technology to provide individualized experiences, expedite customer contacts, and alleviate pain areas because they are aware of the wants and preferences of their customers.

Risk Control and Adherence: When adopting innovative technology, leaders give compliance and risk management priority. They guarantee that technological endeavors conform to industry norms and guidelines, thereby reducing possible hazards and fostering confidence among interested parties.

Constantly Observing Technological Trends: The world of technology is changing quickly. By putting in place systems for ongoing observation of technological developments, leaders help their companies stay ahead of the curve and proactively spot new areas for innovation.

Talent Development and Recruitment: In order to create a workforce with knowledge of future technology, leaders spend on talent development and recruitment techniques. This entails bringing on fresh talent with the ability to spearhead technical innovation and upskilling current staff members.

This exploration shows the strategic significance of utilizing new technology to sustain a competitive edge. As we move forward, we will examine useful tactics that highlight the effective application of developing technology in many industries.

6.3 Mitigating Risks and Ethical Considerations in Innovation

This section focuses on leaders' proactive approaches to managing the risks and ethical issues related to innovation. These include:

Thorough risk evaluation:
Before launching any innovation endeavor, leaders carry out a comprehensive risk assessment. In order to create risk-reduction plans, it is necessary to identify any possible financial, operational, and reputational risks connected to the invention.

Teams for Cross-Functional Risk Management:
Leaders form cross-functional teams devoted to risk management. These teams, which include specialists from different departments, are able to evaluate and handle innovation-related risks from a broad standpoint by combining their expertise.

Strategies for Agile Risk Mitigation:
Because innovation is dynamic, flexible risk-reduction techniques are needed. Effective leaders cultivate adaptable strategies that enable firms to handle unforeseen obstacles and uncertainty effectively.

Creation of an Ethical Framework:
The creation of an ethical framework for innovation is a top priority for leaders. Through the establishment of the organization's guiding principles and values, this framework ensures ethical considerations are factored during decision-making.

Involving stakeholders:
It is crucial to interact with stakeholders in order to comprehend the

many viewpoints on ethical issues. Effective leaders cultivate transparent communication with staff, clients, authorities, and other stakeholders to guarantee that ethical issues are sufficiently attended to.

Consistent Ethical Audits:
Leaders conduct routine ethical audits to evaluate how innovation affects different stakeholders and to spot any possible ethical transgressions. These audits facilitate the continuous improvement of ethical standards and procedures.

Legal Adherence:
Leaders make sure that innovation projects abide by the law. This entails keeping abreast of pertinent legislation and proactively modifying innovative tactics to conform to the legal frameworks of various jurisdictions or sectors.

Communication and Transparency:
Clear communication is essential when addressing moral issues. Open communication is a hallmark of leaders. They discuss the risks that could arise from innovation and the steps taken to reduce them. Transparency helps stakeholders trust one another.

Instruction on Ethical Conduct:
Executives offer staff training courses that highlight the value of moral behavior in innovation. By completing this program, all employees of the company will be guaranteed to comprehend the ethical framework and their responsibility for maintaining ethical standards.

Ongoing Education and Adjustment:
The ethical environment is ever-changing, necessitating ongoing education and adjustment. Leaders cultivate a culture of learning by motivating groups to be aware of new ethical issues and make

proactive adjustments to approaches in order to deal with them.

This investigation sheds light on the proactive measures that leaders can take to maintain moral principles and reduce risks during the innovation process. As we move forward, we will examine the use of case studies and instances that demonstrate ethical issues and effective risk mitigation in a variety of creative scenarios.

7 CASE STUDIES IN INNOVATIVE LEADERSHIP

7.1 Analyzing Success Stories of Executives Who Revolutionized Their Companies

This section focuses on examining the success stories of leaders who have effectively used creative thinking and effective leadership to alter their organizations. They include the following:

Visionary Guidance: Leaders with a visionary approach are frequently featured in success stories. These leaders inspire people to pursue excellence and welcome innovation by articulating a compelling vision that is in line with the goals of the company.

Implementing Strategic Innovation: By looking at success stories, leaders can identify those who deliberately carried out innovative efforts. These leaders approached innovation thoughtfully, whether it was by establishing cross-functional teams, embracing innovative technologies, or fostering a creative culture.

Capability to Adjust: Effective leaders have a high degree of flexibility in response to change. They maneuver through the intricacies of changing consumer expectations, technical environments, and market dynamics, adapting organizational methods to take on fresh difficulties head-on.

Skillful Interaction: A common element in success stories is communication. Successful leaders are able to clearly convey their goals, innovative tactics, and the reasoning behind changes to the organization. Members of a team that communicate clearly and openly are more understanding and aligned.

Encouraging Groups: Success story leaders gave their teams more authority. They gave team members liberty, promoted taking calculated risks, and created a collaborative atmosphere that made them feel important and inspired to give their all to the success of the company.

Strategic Risk Management: Leaders who successfully controlled risks are frequently included in success stories. They carried out in-depth risk assessments, created flexible plans for mitigating risks, and faced uncertainty head-on. Efficient risk management is essential for long-term success.

The Principles of Ethical Leadership: Leaders who gave ethical considerations top priority can be identified by looking at success stories. They created moral frameworks, spoke with stakeholders, and made sure their cutting-edge methods complied with moral requirements. Morally sound leadership builds credibility and trust over time.

Culture of Continuous Learning: Those in charge of success stories promoted a culture of ongoing education. They supported teams in keeping up with industry developments, encouraged skill development, and embraced a growth mindset that views learning as an ongoing part of the organizational journey.

Customer-focused strategies: Effective leaders recognize the value of putting the needs of their customers first. In addition to providing individualized experiences and putting methods into practice to better understand client needs, they also used innovation to develop goods and services that appealed to their target market.

Measurable Results and Adaptation: Leaders who prioritize quantifiable results are frequently the hallmarks of success tales; they monitored performance, established precise KPIs, and modified their plans in response to the findings. The secret to ongoing improvement is the capacity to assess success and make adjustments as necessary.

Examining success stories offers insightful information on the traits, tactics, and organizational transformation-promoting activities of effective leadership. As we move forward, we will examine particular issues in order to draw conclusions and identify principles that leaders may use in their situations.

7.2 Lessons from Failures: Resilience and Adaptability

This section focuses on examining the lessons that can be learned from mistakes, emphasizing the fortitude and flexibility displayed by leaders who encountered difficulties: They include:

Adopting a Growth Perspective: It's common for leaders to adopt a growth mentality after experiencing setbacks. Setbacks are recognized as chances for growth and learning, and they cultivate an environment where obstacles are accepted as a necessary component of the creative process.

An Iterative Method for Innovation: Innovation requires an iterative process in order to learn from mistakes. Effective leaders know that trying new things is important and that not all of their attempts will be successful. They push teams to improve, hone, and adjust in response to input and results.

Open communication regarding setbacks: Effective leaders own up to their mistakes and learn from them. They engage in honest communication with their teams, owning up to errors and offering clarification on the lessons discovered. Open communication fosters trust and facilitates group learning.

Quick Adjustment to Changing Situations: Resilient leaders show quick adjustments to shifting conditions. They are aware of how dynamic the business environment is, and they proactively modify their plans in response to changing consumer preferences, market dynamics, and technological breakthroughs.

Fostering an Environment That Is Safe to Fail: Businesses that grow from their mistakes frequently encourage a culture where mistakes are acceptable. Leaders foster an environment where team members are at ease taking measured risks because they understand that setbacks are seen as learning experiences rather than as punishment.

Examining the Basic Reasons for Failures: Analyzing the underlying causes in depth is necessary for learning from mistakes. In order to avoid future failures of this kind, leaders conduct in-depth analyses of the reasons for the failure of specific initiatives, pinpointing underlying problems and putting corrective measures in place.

Adaptability in the Face of Misfortune: In the midst of difficulty, resilient leaders exhibit poise and grit. They approach obstacles with a positive outlook, motivating their teams to remain committed to long-term objectives and have faith in the company's capacity to overcome setbacks.

Promoting a Culture of Learning: Businesses that grow from their mistakes foster a culture of learning. By offering tools for skill development and fostering chances for teams to exchange knowledge and experiences, leaders actively promote lifelong learning.

Finding a Balance Between Taking and Managing Risks: Effective risk management is implemented by leaders while also promoting risk-taking. They make sure teams have the resources and assistance they need to manage and minimize any potential drawbacks because they recognize that innovation entails measured risks.

Development of Iterative Leadership: Leadership growth is not exempt from learning from mistakes. To effectively guide their teams through both successes and failures, resilient leaders constantly hone their leadership skills through experience, feedback, and approach adaptation.

Learning from mistakes is a great way to gain valuable insights that support organizational flexibility and resilience. As we move forward, we will see important conclusions from situations in which leaders successfully transformed setbacks into teaching moments and chances for personal development.

8 ASSESSING AND QUANTIFYING THE IMPACT OF INNOVATION

8.1 Creating Innovation-Related Key Performance Indicators

This section focuses on creating efficient Key Performance Indicators (KPIs) that are specially designed to gauge and evaluate how well innovation is implemented inside a company. They comprise:

Consistency with Strategic Goals:

Innovation KPIs need to be closely aligned with the strategic goals of the firm. They ought to demonstrate how innovation advances overarching objectives, guaranteeing that the search for fresh concepts and inventive solutions is in line with the larger purpose.

Measurable Indicators:

KPIs that work are measurable. They give leaders quantifiable information so they can monitor advancement and assess the results of innovative projects. Measurable metrics are useful in evaluating the volume and caliber of inventive outputs.

Metrics for Innovation Output:

KPIs ought to gauge the results of innovation. This could be the quantity of newly introduced goods or services, the accomplishment of process enhancements, the number of patents submitted, or other observable results of creative endeavors.

Time-to-Market Efficiency:

Time-to-market efficiency is a critical KPI for innovation. It evaluates the speed at which novel concepts are developed into goods or services that are ready for the market. Effective time-to-market is frequently a good indicator of how flexible and responsive a company is.

Impact and Satisfaction with Customers:

KPIs ought to assess how innovation affects clients. This could include gathering input on the perceived value of novel solutions, monitoring client adoption rates, or gauging consumer happiness with new offers.

Staff Involvement in Innovation:

One useful KPI that measures how much staff participates actively in the innovation process is employee engagement. A few examples of metrics are the quantity of ideas that are submitted, attendance at innovation workshops, and usage of innovation platforms.

ROI vs. innovation cost:

Economy of scale is essential. KPIs ought to evaluate how much innovation efforts cost in relation to their ROI (return on investment). This sheds light on the effectiveness of resource distribution as well as the overall financial results of innovation initiatives.

Rate of Learning and Experimentation:

One suggestive KPI is the rate of exploration and learning. It gauges how rapidly the company tries out new concepts, learns from results (both good and bad), and modifies plans in response to these insights.

Metrics for Cross-Functional Collaboration:

The degree of cross-functional cooperation in innovation should be reflected in KPIs. The success of cross-functional teams, the frequency of departmental collaboration, or the variety of skill sets incorporated into innovation projects are a few examples of valuable metrics.

Taking Up Novel Approaches:

It's critical to monitor how the company embraces new practices. KPIs in this area could track how well new technologies are integrated, how inventive problems are solved, or how innovative methodologies are applied across a range of company operations.

Feedback Loop Effectiveness:

Smart KPIs evaluate the innovation process's feedback loop. This entails gauging the effectiveness of the processes used to gather, evaluate, and incorporate feedback from stakeholders, including consumers, staff members, and other parties.

Creating strong KPIs for innovation guarantees that the company has a systematic framework for assessing and enhancing its innovation capacities. As we move on, we will examine instances that demonstrate how innovation KPIs have been successfully implemented in various corporate contexts.

8.2 Balancing Short-Term Outcomes with Long-Term Goals

In the framework of organizational innovation, this section focuses on striking a careful balance between sustaining a long-term goal and obtaining immediate results. This can be done through:

Strategic Alignment:

Strategic alignment is the first step towards balancing immediate outcomes with a long-term vision. By ensuring that short-term decisions are in line with the organization's larger vision, leaders avoid situations where short-term objectives and long-term viability collide.

Prioritizing Innovation Portfolios:

Leaders strategically prioritize innovation portfolios. They make a distinction between efforts that help achieve long-term strategic goals and those that produce rapid victories to show value right away. This order of importance guarantees a fair strategy.

Quickly completing short-term objectives:

Agility is used in the execution of short-term goals. Effective leaders foster an organizational culture that allows for swift adaptation to dynamic market conditions and ensures that short-term initiatives do not impede the organization's long-term objectives.

Investment in future capabilities:

Making deliberate investments in future skills is necessary to balance short-term results. Leaders commit funds to projects that might not pay off right away, but they help the company become more innovative and competitive over the long term.

Keeping an eye on KPIs, or key performance indicators:

KPIs must be continuously observed. In order to ensure that innovation initiatives are visible in the short term and that they are in line with the organization's long-term strategic goals, leaders monitor both short- and long-term KPIs.

Motivation and Recognition of Employees:

Keeping a balance requires acknowledging and inspiring employees. In addition to offering encouragement and support, leaders recognize and celebrate short-term victories and emphasize their significance within the larger, long-term goal.

Vision Communication:

Leaders convey the organization's long-term vision consistently. This guarantees that workers comprehend the greater intention underlying immediate activities, promoting a sense of purpose and dedication to the organization's overall objectives.

A roadmap for innovation with milestones:

Both short- and long-term goals are included in a well-defined innovation roadmap. This plan helps the organization stay on track to accomplish transformative, long-term results while guiding it through urgent problems.

Risk Reduction and Flexibility:

It takes both flexibility and efficient risk management to balance immediate outcomes. When taking quick action, leaders foresee possible hazards and make sure plans are in place to reduce those risks without jeopardizing the organization's long-term sustainability.

Ongoing Assessment and Modification:

Leaders assess and modify their plans on a regular basis. They understand that striking a balance between immediate outcomes and long-term goals is a dynamic process that may call for recalibration in response to changes in the business environment or new opportunities.

This section emphasizes how crucial it is to have a strategic and nuanced approach when it comes to organizational innovation in order to strike a balance between immediate outcomes and long-term goals. As we move further, we will see examples that demonstrate effective methods for striking this fine balance.

8.3 Significance of Iteration and Feedback in Continuous Improvement

Understanding the critical roles that iteration and feedback play in the ongoing development of organizational innovation is the main goal of this section. These comprise:

Perpetual Feedback Loops: Feedback loops are essential to ongoing development. Organizations set up mechanisms to collect feedback from stakeholders, such customers and employees, during the innovation process. These loops provide areas for improvement as well as the efficacy of the current tactics.

Analytics and real-time monitoring: Analytics and real-time monitoring are essential. Businesses utilize technology to monitor user behavior, performance indicators, and other pertinent data in real-time. Decisions are informed by this instant feedback, which also allows for quick adjustments to maximize innovative activities.

Client input as a motivator: Iteration is primarily driven by customer feedback. Businesses place a high priority on learning about consumers' experiences using their goods and services. This input directs the creation of customer-centric innovations in addition to pointing out areas that require improvement.

Employee Collaboration and Input: Employee feedback is a great place to start. Businesses foster a culture where employees feel free to express their thoughts, opinions, and concerns. Working together across teams guarantees a variety of perspectives, which strengthens the results of innovation.

Iterative testing and prototyping: Testing and iterative prototyping are essential steps in the innovation process. Minimum viable products, or MVPs, are developed by organizations and then tested and improved upon in response to user input. Before a full-scale launch, ongoing improvement is possible with this iterative strategy.

Agile Methodologies for Development: Agile development approaches place a strong emphasis on iteration and ongoing feedback. Agile techniques enable organizations to arrange their innovation processes flexibly, enabling quick alterations in response to feedback obtained throughout brief development cycles.

Taking lessons from mistakes: Organizations see failures as chances to improve and learn rather than seeing them as obstacles. Leaders urge their people to examine what went wrong, identify the underlying reasons, and refine their approach. This learning-oriented culture supports ongoing development.

Making Decisions Based on Data: Using data to inform decisions is essential to ongoing development. Businesses examine information from a range of sources, such as performance indicators, market trends, and consumer interactions. Data insights guide strategic decisions and the continual improvement of innovation initiatives.

Models of Scalable Innovation: Models for scalable innovation allow for ongoing progress. Businesses create scalable innovation frameworks that enable the replication and iterative improvement of successful strategies across several divisions or business units.

Including Feedback in Strategic Planning: Input is incorporated into strategy planning rather than being gathered separately. Organizations use feedback mechanisms to gather insights that help them align their strategic goals. This guarantees that the process of continuous improvement has a purpose and advances the overall goals of the company.

This investigation highlights how feedback and iteration are interwoven within an organization's overall innovation strategy rather than existing as separate processes. As we move further, we'll examine cases that demonstrate how feedback and iteration may be effectively applied to promote continuous improvement in a range of organizational contexts.

9 MAINTAINING A CREATIVE CULTURE

9.1 Integrating Creativity into Organizational Culture

This section centers on the strategic method for integrating innovation as a fundamental component of the corporate DNA. This can be achieved through the following:

Cultural Transformation:

A shift in culture is required to integrate innovation. A culture that encourages innovation, curiosity, and a readiness to question the status quo is fostered by leaders. The cornerstone for integrating innovation into the organization's operations is this cultural transformation.

Dedication to Leadership:

Leadership dedication is essential. Top-level executives and leaders show a strong commitment to innovation by supporting and actively engaging in creative projects. Their dedication sets the standard for the entire company.

Clearly defined goals and plans:

A well-defined vision and innovation strategy guide the transition. A compelling vision that explains the importance of innovation and how it fits with the organization's long-term goals is articulated by leaders. A clearly defined strategy provides an implementation roadmap.

All-encompassing innovation:

Inclusivity is necessary for integrating creativity. Businesses understand that creative ideas can originate from any department or level. In order to ensure that a variety of viewpoints are included in the innovation process, leaders provide inclusive venues for the creation of ideas.

Ongoing Education and Training:

Ongoing education and growth take center stage. Companies make investments in projects and programs that help workers develop their skills and capacities, creating a workforce that can both contribute to and flourish in an innovative setting.

Allocating Resources to Innovation:

It's crucial to allocate resources appropriately. Organizations allot budgetary resources, personnel, and time to support innovation projects. This pledge highlights the value of innovation and offers the assistance required for the creation and application of fresh concepts.

Agile Procedures and Structures:

Implementing agile structures and procedures is a prerequisite for embedding innovation. Flexible organizational structures enable prompt decision-making, experimentation, and adaptation. Agile methods take into account how dynamic the invention process is.

Recognition and Rewards for Innovation:

Systems of incentives and recognition are in line with the objectives of innovation. Businesses recognize and honor individuals and groups that make substantial contributions to the innovation process. This acknowledgment highlights how important creative efforts are.

Platforms and Tools for Collaboration:

Tools and platforms for collaboration are incorporated into regular business processes. Organizations utilize digital platforms to enable inter-team communication, idea-sharing, and collaboration. These tools improve cross-functional collaboration and expedite the invention process.

Feedback Systems:

Sturdy feedback systems have been put in place. Companies design methodical procedures for gathering, evaluating, and responding to stakeholder and employee input. The iterative feedback loop plays a pivotal role in the enhancement and optimization of innovative techniques.

Organizational Learning from Failures:

The organizational philosophy is deeply rooted in learning from mistakes. Organizations perceive failures as chances to develop, learn, and adapt rather than as setbacks. In the process of innovation, leaders convey the value of resiliency and learning from mistakes.

Integration of ecosystems and strategic partnerships:

Companies look for strategic alliances and incorporate them into larger ecosystems. Working with outside organizations, like startups, academic institutions, or business associations, gives access to a variety of viewpoints and resources that promote creativity.

This exploration emphasizes that integrating innovation into the organizational DNA is a thorough and deliberate process that calls for dedication, a shift in the organization's culture, and strategic alignment with all divisions. We will examine more examples as we go along to show effective methods for integrating innovation into various organizational settings.

9.2 Leadership Succession: Maintaining Creative Leadership Continuity

The strategic factors and procedures to guarantee a smooth leadership transition that upholds continuity while encouraging creative and innovative leadership will be covered in this section. They comprise of:

Determining the Essential Leadership Qualities:

The first step in a successful leadership succession plan is identifying the essential leadership qualities linked to innovation and creativity. Organizations identify the fundamental abilities and characteristics needed to foster innovation and look for these qualities in possible successors.

Programs for Leadership Development:

Businesses fund initiatives aimed at developing leaders. The goal of these programs is to develop a pipeline of leaders who have a strong focus on innovation and creativity. Training is provided to participants to improve their leadership skills in creative and dynamic work settings.

Transfer of knowledge and mentoring:

A key component of leadership succession is mentoring. Enthusiastic and innovative leaders guide prospective heirs by imparting wisdom, experiences, and insights. This mentorship ensures that the creative vision and methodology are successfully transferred, facilitating a seamless transition.

Succession Planning for Creativity:

Creativity is particularly included as a crucial criterion in succession planning. Businesses aggressively seek out people who have creative potential and develop them for leadership positions. This tactical method guarantees that a pool of talent exists that is prepared to assume innovative leadership roles.

Making Innovation Processes Institutional:

Organizations institutionalize innovation processes to guarantee continuity. Instead of depending only on certain individuals, they create institutions, processes, and frameworks that encourage creativity. By ensuring that innovation is ingrained in the company culture, this strategy helps to minimize disruptions during changes in leadership.

Diversity in the Succession of Leadership:

The emphasis of leadership succession plans is on diversity. Companies make sure that the pool of possible leaders includes people with a variety of backgrounds, skills, and skill sets because they understand the importance of many viewpoints in fostering creativity.

Perpetual Assessment of Leadership Potential:

Organizations assess leadership potential on a constant basis. This entails continuous evaluations of each person's effectiveness, flexibility, and compatibility with the organization's principles and objectives for innovation. Regular evaluations influence decisions about succession and leadership development.

Open Communication Regarding Succession:

Open communication is essential. Organizations make sure that staff members are aware of the company's dedication to supporting innovative leadership and the procedures in place for smooth transitions by being transparent about their leadership succession plans.

Promoting a Learning Culture:

Effective leadership succession requires a culture of learning. Companies create an atmosphere where leaders—both established and emerging—are dedicated to lifelong learning. This culture makes sure that executives remain up-to-date with changing trends and obstacles in the field of innovation.

Establishing a Pipeline for Leadership:

Companies work hard to create a pipeline of future leaders. This entails locating and fostering people who demonstrate creative leadership potential at various levels. Establishing a strong pipeline guarantees a consistent flow of creative leaders as the company develops.

Flexibility and adaptability:

Plans for leadership transition include a strong emphasis on flexibility and adaptation. Organizations make sure that succession plans are flexible enough to accommodate changes based on new needs since they understand that the business environment and innovation requirements might fluctuate.

Systems for managing knowledge:

Systems for managing knowledge contribute to continuity. Systems that collect and arrange important information about innovation are put into place by organizations. These systems facilitate the transmission of tacit knowledge from departing leaders to their successors.

This enquiry demonstrates that a proactive and comprehensive strategy is needed for creative leadership in order to ensure effective leadership succession. Organizations may guarantee the continuation of a creative leadership legacy by incorporating creativity into succession planning and putting knowledge transfer and continuous learning initiatives into practice. We will see more examples that demonstrate effective leadership succession strategies for imaginative and creative leadership as we move forward.

9.3 Honoring and Acknowledging Ingenuity: The Influence of Positive Feedback

This section aims to clarify the importance of acknowledging and appreciating innovation as a potent tool for positive reinforcement in the workplace culture. This entails:

Reinforcement of Culture: Recognizing and applauding creativity is a potent way to reinforce culture. The celebration of inventive accomplishments by firms fosters an innovation-centric culture by sending a strong message that creativity is respected and rewarded.

Engagement and Motivation of Employees: Employee engagement and motivation are boosted by positive reinforcement via celebration. Acknowledging innovative initiatives in the workplace with prizes, commendations, or public recognition improves morale and motivates staff to participate in the organization's innovation agenda actively.

Presenting inspiring figures: Celebrations offer a chance to highlight innovative role models. Organizations may foster an innovative culture by showcasing the people or groups responsible for significant innovations. This establishes recognizable role models that encourage others to seek out original ideas and contribute to the organization's innovative culture.

Fostering a Feeling of Belonging: Honoring creativity promotes a sense of community. Employee loyalty to the company is increased when they see their creative ideas valued and appreciated. The sense of community this foster increases worker loyalty and satisfaction.

Highlighting Achievements: Sharing success stories with the public helps to convey the value of innovation. Businesses communicate success stories both internally and externally to highlight how creative ideas have solved problems or opened up new avenues. Additionally, the organization's standing as a creative leader is strengthened by this external communication.

Official Recognition Initiatives: Creating official recognition initiatives is a systematic process. Programs that explicitly acknowledge and reward creative contributions are implemented by organizations. This could take the form of honors, financial incentives, or chances for professional advancement connected to productive innovation outcomes.

Creating a Positive Feedback Cycle: Festivities support a positive feedback cycle. When workers are acknowledged for their creative efforts, it serves to instill further the belief that their contributions are important. In turn, this encouraging feedback promotes ongoing participation in the creative process.

Matching recognition to fundamental values: Recognition initiatives are in line with basic principles. Businesses make sure that awards and celebrations align with the principles that guide their innovation strategy. This alignment strengthens the relationship between innovation and the organization's overarching goals and values.

Collaborative Innovation Team Celebrations: Highlights include group accomplishments. The recognition of collaborative innovation emphasizes the significance of cooperation and cross-functional collaboration in the innovation process. Celebrations among teammates foster a sense of unity and accomplishment.

Constant Feedback Systems: Festivities are a component of ongoing feedback systems. Celebrations are included in routine feedback loops by organizations to guarantee that creative efforts are recognized promptly and consistently. Celebrations on a regular basis foster a culture of continuous reinforcement.

Innovation Events and Showcases: Organizing events and showcases of innovation provides a forum for public celebration. Organizations arrange events showcasing creative projects, goods, or concepts. These gatherings encourage people to pursue excellence in innovation and act as a platform for communal celebration.

Personalized Acknowledgment for Diverse Contributions: Efforts to recognize different kinds of contributions are customized. In order to accommodate the variety of contributions, organizations acknowledge and celebrate different facets of the innovation journey, whether it's a ground-breaking concept, a successful implementation, or a resilient reaction to failure.

Organizations can instill a culture where innovation is cherished, celebrated, and integrated into everyday operations by recognizing and utilizing the power of positive reinforcement through celebrations and recognition. As we go along, we'll look at particular instances that show effective methods for honoring and celebrating innovation.

10 LOOKING AHEAD: UPCOMING DEVELOPMENTS IN INNOVATION AND LEADERSHIP

10.1 The Intersection of Sustainability, Innovation, and Leadership

This section delves into the deep relationship that exists between sustainability,

innovation, and leadership, highlighting the ways in which these three factors

work together to create long-term success and good effects:

Sustainable Innovation Leadership: A key factor in promoting sustainable innovation is leadership. Visionary leaders understand how critical it is to coordinate innovative initiatives with environmentally friendly behaviors. They lead their companies in creating creative solutions that advance social and environmental sustainability in addition to business goals.

Strategic Integration of Sustainability: Enterprises that achieve success include sustainability in their overarching business plan. It is the responsibility of leaders to make sure that sustainability is integrated into all facets of the business, impacting operational procedures, product creation, and decision-making.

Creative Remedies for Environmental Problems: Leaders spark innovative approaches to solving environmental problems. This involves adopting technology that lessens the damaging effects of corporate activities on the ecosystem, creating ecologically friendly products, and putting sustainable supply chain practices in place.

Socially Responsible Leadership: Social responsibility is a component of leadership in the context of sustainability. Initiatives that benefit society, such as charitable work, moral business conduct, and community involvement, are supported by leaders. Sustainable and moral corporate practices are compatible with socially responsible Leadership.

The Triple Bottom Line Method: Businesses use a triple-bottom-line strategy, taking into account environmental, social, and economic aspects. Leaders understand that sustainable innovation is not just about making money. They strive for a balance that is advantageous to all stakeholders and gauge success based on its effects on people, the environment, and profitability.

The long-term vision for resilient organizations: The goal of sustainable leadership is to create resilient organizations over the long run. Leaders are aware that tackling social and environmental issues is not only morally right but also helps the company remain viable and flexible over the long run in a changing global context.

Offering Incentives for Green Practices: Green practices are encouraged throughout the organization by leaders. This could entail recognizing environmentally friendly activities, rewarding sustainable accomplishments, and fostering an environment where staff members are motivated to support the company's sustainability objectives.

Eco-Innovation: An important component of the intersection is eco-innovation. Eco-innovation, or creating goods, services, and procedures with a smaller environmental impact, is embraced by companies with sustainable leadership. Leaders foster a culture of continuous progress toward more sustainable practices.

Circular Economy Models: Executives investigate and apply circular economy concepts. This entails minimizing waste, developing closed-loop systems, and designing items with recycling and reuse in mind. Practices in the circular economy promote responsible resource management and are consistent with the concepts of sustainable leadership.

Coping with Climate Change: Leaders deal with the effects of climate change in a proactive manner. Understanding and reducing the consequences of climate change on the company's operations, supply chain, and local communities are all part of sustainable leadership. Initiatives to lower carbon emissions and boost resilience are also paramount.

Involving stakeholders in sustainability: Establishing connections with stakeholders is a key component of sustainable leadership. This entails working together to achieve sustainable goals with vendors, clients, and neighborhood communities. Collaboration and open communication create a network of support for sustainable projects.

Regulation, Adherence, and Moral Principles: Sustainable leaders maintain moral principles and make sure that environmental laws are followed. They understand the significance of acting morally and according to the law regarding the environment. The company's social responsibility and reputation are enhanced by this dedication to compliance.

Assessing and Reporting the Impact of Sustainability:
Businesses with a sustainable leadership model track and openly
share their sustainability impact. This entails monitoring key
performance metrics pertaining to social and environmental
sustainability and regularly updating stakeholders on the
organization's advancement toward sustainability objectives.

Organizations looking to build long-lasting value must comprehend
how sustainability, innovation, and leadership connect.
Organizations may ensure long-term profitability while promoting
positive social and environmental effects by embracing responsible
leadership and incorporating sustainable practices into innovative
initiatives. As we move further, we will look at examples that show
effective strategies at this intersection.

10.2: How International Trends and Events Affect Leadership Practices

This section delves into the ways in which global events and trends
impact leadership practices, influencing how leaders approach
obstacles, promote creativity, and propel organizational success.
They entail:

The global landscape is dynamic.
The world landscape is dynamic due in part to global trends and
occurrences. Rapid changes in the world of leadership are
commonplace, including changes in the geopolitical landscape,
upheavals in the economy, advances in technology, and crises in
public health. Effective leadership techniques are essential in this
kind of changing environment.

Crisis management and adaptability:
Adaptive leadership is necessary in times of crisis, be it a global

epidemic, an economic downturn, or geopolitical tensions. Leaders need to be able to bounce back from setbacks, act quickly, and handle uncertainty. Crisis management entails guiding the company through difficulties, preserving stability, and guaranteeing the welfare of the workforce.

Work from Home and Dispersed Teams:

Global trends have an impact on leadership techniques, such as the growing popularity of remote work. Leaders must adopt digital collaboration tools, foster a culture of mutual respect, and effectively manage remote teams if they are to flourish in virtual work environments.

Focus on Diverse and Inclusive Leadership:

World events have heightened the significance of inclusive and diverse leadership. Leaders understand the importance of inclusivity and a range of viewpoints when making decisions. In reaction to social pressures, organizations place a high value on building diverse leadership teams with a range of experiences, backgrounds, and viewpoints.

Advancements in Technology:

Quick changes in technology influence leadership styles. Leaders use evolving technologies to boost productivity, stimulate creativity, and maintain their competitive edge. Understanding and judiciously applying technology, such as blockchain, data analytics, and artificial intelligence are hallmarks of tech-savvy leadership.

Social and Environmental Responsibility:

World events that affect leadership practices toward environmental and social responsibility include social justice movements and knowledge of climate change. Leaders acknowledge that social issues and company principles must be harmonized. They also employ sustainable techniques.

Taking Geopolitics into Account:
Events in geopolitics affect international business activities. While navigating the complexities of geopolitics, leaders take trade agreements, diplomatic alliances, and geopolitical dangers into account. Planning scenarios, controlling risks, and keeping an international viewpoint on the company strategy are all components of adaptive leadership.

Well-being of Employees and Public Health:
The continued effects of public health incidents, such as pandemics, have made employee well-being more important. To create a resilient and healthy corporate culture, leaders put their employees' health and safety first, offer flexible work schedules, and assist with mental health programs.

Management of Change and Agility:
Events around the world need a greater emphasis on change management and agility. Organizations need their leaders to guide them through constant adaptation to outside circumstances. Agile leadership approaches are welcoming to change, creativity, and making sure teams are able to react quickly to changing conditions.

International Cooperation and Alliances:
Leaders understand the value of international cooperation and alliances. Events and trends on a global scale highlight the globalization of business. Leaders form strategic alliances, partnerships, and collaborations in order to take advantage of group strengths and tackle common issues.

A Closer Look at Ethical Leadership:
The accent is on ethical leadership in light of current world issues. It is expected of leaders to respect moral principles, convey choices openly and honestly, and give stakeholders' needs top priority. In

unpredictable times, trust and resilience are strengthened by ethical leadership behaviors.

Taking note of international best practices:
Global best practices provide valuable insights for leaders. Because the globe is interconnected, leaders can benefit from successful strategies used in other businesses and geographical areas. This thought exchange helps to create a more knowledgeable and flexible leadership style.

For leaders, to effectively manage challenging and quickly evolving settings, must have a thorough understanding of how global trends and events affect their leadership practices. Through the use of flexible tactics, giving attention to workers' welfare, and standing by moral and sustainable values, executives can set up their companies for long-term success in a changing global environment. As we go along, we'll look at examples of successful leadership reactions to various trends and events around the world.

10.3 The Ongoing Evolution of the Leadership-Innovation Nexus

This section delves into the dynamic and ever-evolving relationship between innovation and leadership, highlighting how this relationship is always flexible in response to new problems, advances in technology, and changes in organizational paradigms: This is explained below:

Agile Management for Quick Innovation:
The leadership-innovation nexus now embraces agility. Effective leaders understand that conditions and market demands change quickly. Agile leadership practices emphasize making decisions quickly, using iterative techniques, and being able to change course when new information becomes available.

Focus on collaborative and inclusive leadership:
Collaboration and inclusivity are at the center of the changing nexus. Leaders know that diverse, team-oriented settings foster creativity. Embracing a culture of open communication, appreciating different points of view, and giving teams the freedom to participate in the creative process are all components of inclusive leadership approaches.

Using Technology in Leadership Positions:
Technology is becoming a crucial part of leadership techniques. Advanced technologies, including automation, data analytics, and artificial intelligence, are used by leaders to boost innovation, improve operational efficiency, and influence decision-making. A key component of tech-savvy leadership is the ongoing incorporation of developing technology.

The mindset of Entrepreneurial Leadership:
An entrepreneurial attitude influences the relationship between leadership and innovation. Entrepreneurial mindsets are adopted by leaders who embrace risk, promote experimentation, and see obstacles as chances for creativity. A resilient and creative culture is fostered by entrepreneurial leadership.

A Transition to Servant Leadership:
There is a change in the evolving nexus toward servant leadership. Serving the needs of their teams, empowering staff members, and fostering an atmosphere where people can provide their finest ideas are all top priorities for leaders. A sense of purpose and dedication to the objectives of the company are fostered by servant leadership.

Data-Informed Decision-Making in Innovation:
Making decisions based on data are a fundamental component of the changing nexus. Leaders use data analytics to monitor performance,

find areas for improvement, and inform innovation efforts. This data-driven strategy improves the accuracy and efficiency of innovation projects.

Human-Centric Innovation Leadership:
Innovation approaches place a strong emphasis on human-centric leadership. Leaders know how important it is to comprehend and meet the demands of their team members, clients, and other stakeholders. A culture of empathy, creativity, and user-focused innovation is fostered by human-centric leadership.

Continuous Education and Adaptation:
The dynamic nexus places a high value on ongoing learning and adjustment. Leaders are aware that continuing organizational and personal development is necessary to stay ahead of the innovation curve. Adopting fresh ideas, abilities, and information is a key component of learning-oriented leadership.

Purpose-Driven Leadership for Sustainable Innovation:
The developing nexus has purpose-driven leadership as a major theme. The influence of innovations on societal and environmental well-being is emphasized by leaders who link innovation activities with a purpose. Organizations are guided toward meaningful and sustainable innovation by purpose-driven leadership.

Adaptability and Hardiness in Leadership Approaches:
Leadership philosophies have evolved to be more adaptable and durable. Understanding that a one-size-fits-all leadership style might not work in the varied and dynamic world of innovation, leaders modify their methods to meet the situation. A key component of resilient leadership is fast strategy adjustment and learning from mistakes.

Ecosystem Leadership for Collaborative Innovation:

Ecosystem leadership is emphasized in the emerging nexus. Leaders know how important it is to work together with startups, outside partners, and other players in the innovation ecosystem. Building and fostering cooperative networks is a key component of ecosystem leadership in order to stimulate group creativity.

Ethical Leadership in Innovation Governance:

A crucial factor in the governance of innovation is ethical leadership. A strong ethical compass is used by leaders to steer firms, making sure that innovation processes comply with legal requirements, social expectations, and ethical norms. Sustainable innovation and trust are fostered by ethical leadership.

It is essential for leaders navigating the intricacies of the contemporary corporate world to comprehend the ongoing evolution of the leadership-innovation nexus. Through the adoption of agile, inclusive, tech-integrated, and ethical practices, executives can cultivate an innovative
culture that drives their companies toward long-term success. As we go along, we'll look at areas that show off successful leadership techniques at the dynamic intersection of innovation and leadership.

Conclusion:

Developing The Future Generation of Innovative Leaders

As we come to the end of our exploration into the relationship between leadership and innovation, our attention turns to developing the next wave of leaders who will propel innovation in the future. Key conclusions and things to think about are as follows:

The Role of Leadership in Creating Innovation:
A strong catalyst for creativity is leadership. Upon contemplation of the different aspects of leadership that this book delves into, it is clear that visionary and flexible leaders are essential to developing a creative culture and propelling revolutionary innovation in companies.

Flexible Leadership in a Changing Environment:

Adaptive leadership is necessary in the modern business environment due to its dynamic character. The skills necessary for navigating uncertainty, leading through crises, and embracing change must be possessed by tomorrow's leaders. The ongoing development of the relationship between leadership and innovation emphasizes how crucial it is to maintain flexibility in the face of new obstacles.

Collaborative and Inclusive Leadership:
Tomorrow's leaders must give inclusion and cooperation top priority. Diverse, cooperative settings that encourage people to share their special viewpoints are conducive to innovation. To fully unleash a team's creative potential, inclusive leadership approaches and a dedication to collaboration is critical.

Leadership with Purpose and Ethics:
A sense of purpose and ethical principles should guide future leaders. When anchored in moral values and a distinct goal, the relationship between leadership and innovation have the greatest potential for effect. For Responsible innovation that is in line with ethical norms and environmental sustainability, tomorrow's leaders must give societal values a top priority.

Ongoing Education and Technological Proficiency:
Developing future leaders requires a dedication to lifelong learning and technological proficiency. Leaders need to keep up with market trends, adopt emerging technology, and make use of data-driven insights. Leaders who adopt a learning-oriented perspective are better prepared to guide in a technological environment that is always changing.

Servant Leadership and Human-Centric Approach:
Approaches that emphasize servant leadership and human centricity are essential. The well-being of their teams should be given top

priority by tomorrow's leaders, who should also work to foster empathy and collaborative and creative cultures. A culture where people are enabled to make significant contributions to the innovation process is fostered by servant leadership.

Leadership that is eco-innovative and sustainable:
Eco-innovation and sustainability need to be fundamental components of leadership techniques. Future leaders will need to coordinate their innovation endeavors with sustainability objectives, embrace environmentally conscious behaviors, and make a constructive contribution to the environment. Innovation that is responsible, long-lasting, and revolutionary is guaranteed by sustainable leadership.

Ecosystem Leadership and a Global View:
Future leaders must possess both a global vision and ecosystem leadership skills. Building cooperative networks, interacting with outside partners, and realizing how intertwined the world's economic landscape is are all necessary for fostering innovation. It is easier for leaders with a global mindset to negotiate the challenges of an interconnected world.

The focus is on developing a comprehensive leadership style that includes adaptability, diversity, ethical considerations, and a dedication to sustainable practices in order to develop tomorrow's innovative leaders. Organizations and leaders who take this path advance not just their success but also the welfare of the planet and society at large. The leadership-innovation nexus is evolving at an exciting and revolutionary rate, and it has the potential to shape a future in which innovation is not only a strategic imperative but also a force for good in the world.

ABOUT THE AUTHOR

Daniel W. Njuguna, a Certified Public Accountant of Kenya and a full member of ICPAK, offers a plethora of expertise in financial management, auditing, accounting, and Lecturing. Over his career, he has held positions in accounting colleges, audit firms, and Saccos. Daniel's dedication to disseminating knowledge from his varied experiences is evident in "Leadership and Innovation: Fostering a Culture of Creativity". This book uses his expertise to give readers more confidence in their ability to lead and innovate. As a seasoned professional, Daniel hopes to contribute to the conversation on good leadership and foster creative organizational cultures while providing readers with a useful tool for development and prosperity.